CW00402851

A STEP BY STEP GUIDE FOR MUSLIM BOYS AND GIRLS

HOW TO PRAY
FOR KIDS

THIS BOOK BELONGS TO

imranimand

khadija

QURAN TRANSLATIONS BY:
DR. MUSTAFA KHATTAB
'THE CLEAR QURÁN'

COURTESY OF WWW.QURAN.COM

© HOUSE OF GUIDANCE | ALL RIGHTS RESERVED

Let's Start with Bismillah

TABLE OF CONTENTS

KEY WORDS/PHRASES

SHAHADA = DECLARATION OF FAITH

SALAH = PRAYER

ZAKAT = ALMSGIVING

SAWM = FASTING

HAJJ = PILGRIMAGE

RAKAAH = UNIT OF PRAYER

RUKU = TO BOW

SUJOOD = PROSTRATION

SURAH = CHAPTER

What is Salah (Prayer)?

SALAH (PRAYER) IS THE SECOND PILLAR OF THE 'FIVE PILLARS' OF ISLAM. THE BELIEF THAT ALL MUSLIMS SHOULD PRAY FIVE TIMES EVERY DAY.

WE PRAY TO WORSHIP ALLAH, TO MAINTAIN OUR FAITH, TO COMMUNICATE WITH OUR CREATOR AND TO DO MORE GOOD DEEDS.

The Five Pillars of Islam

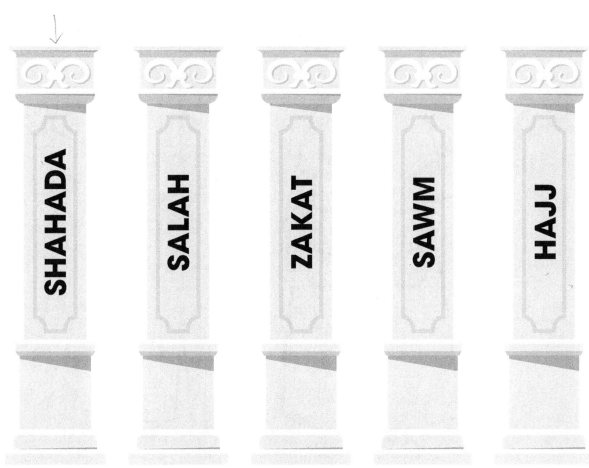

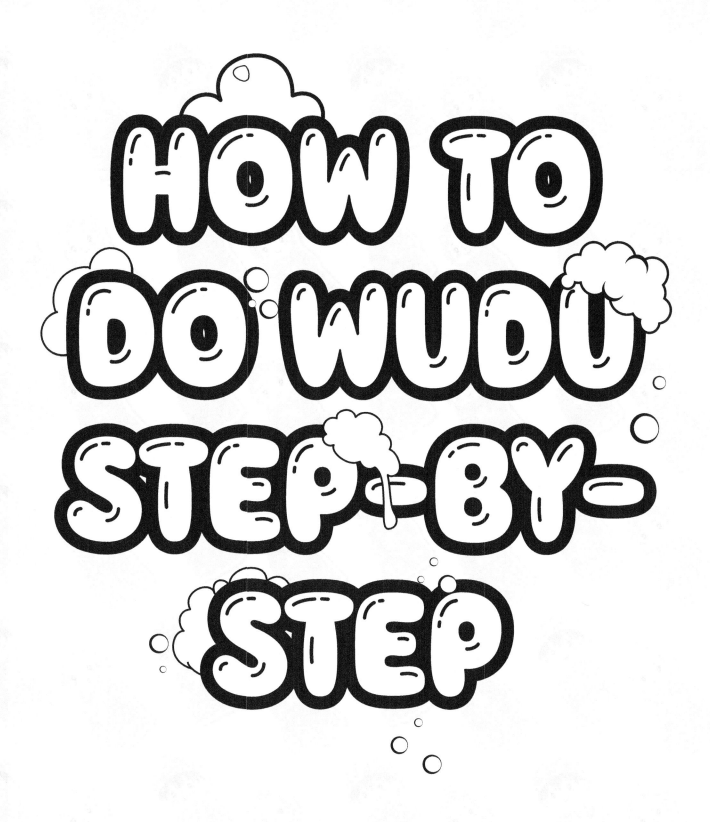

HOW TO DO WUDU STEP-BY-STEP

Step ① Begin by saying Bismillah

Step ② Wash Hands

Wash hands starting from the right hand including wrist and between fingers 3 times.

Step ③ Rinse Mouth

Take a handful of water with your right hand to rinse your mouth 3 times.

Step ④ Clean Nose

Take a handful of water with your right hand, sniff it into your nostrils, and blow it out 3 times

Step ⑤ Wash Face

Wash your face from the hairline to the chin
and from ear to ear 3 times.

Step ⑥ Wash Arms

Wash your arms up to the elbows, starting from the right, 3 times.

14

Step ⑦ Wipe Head

Wipe your head starting from the front all way to the back of the head and back to the front again.

Step ⑧ Clean Ears

Clean the inside grooves of your ears with your finger
and the back with your thumb.

Step ⑨ Wash Feet

Wash feet up to the ankles and between the toes starting from the right foot 3 times.

Did you know?

BOYS AND GIRLS PERFORM WUDU IN THE SAME WAY!

BIG THINGS HAVE SMALL BEGINNINGS

THE FIVE DAILY PRAYERS

We as Muslims pray five times a day and these prayers known as Fajr, Dhuhr, Asr, Maghrib and Isha.

Those prayers differ in the time they are performed, numbers of rakaat and in the recitation whether it's loud or not.

OVERVIEW

A summary of all the daily prayers

PRAYERS	NUMBER OF RAKAAT	SILENT/ALOUD	TIME OF THE DAY
FAJR	2	ALOUD	DAWN (BEFORE SUNRISE)
DHUHR	4	SILENT	MIDDAY
ASR	4	SILENT	MID-AFTERNOON
MAGHRIB	3	1ST & 2ND RAKAAT ALOUD 3RD RAKAAT SILENT	SUNSET
ISHA	4	1ST & 2ND RAKAAT ALOUD 3RD & 4TH RAKAAT SILENT	EVENING

Fajr 2
Maghrib 3

Dhuhr
Asr   4 each
Isha

24

HADITH ON PRAYER

Sayings of Prophet Mohammad (PBUH)

with shine

The Prophet (ﷺ) said, "If there was a river at the door of anyone of you and he took a bath in it five times a day would you notice any dirt on him?"

They said, "Not a trace of dirt would be left."

The Prophet (ﷺ) added, "That is the example of the five prayers with which Allah blots out evil deeds."

(Sahih al-Bukhari)

1. FAJR

2 Rak'aat | Prayer at dawn (before Sunrise)

	Standing	Bowing	Return to Standing	Prostration	Sitting	Return to Prostration	Return to Sitting
Rak'ah (1)							
Rak'ah (2)							

At the end of the prayer, turn your face to the right then left and say the Salaam

2. DHUHR

4 Rak'aat | Prayer at midday

	Standing	Bowing	Return to Standing	Prostration	Sitting	Return to Prostration	Return to Sitting
Rak'ah (1)							
Rak'ah (2)							
Rak'ah (3)							
Rak'ah (4)							

At the end of the prayer, turn your face to the right then left and say the Salaam

3. ASR

4 Rak'aat | Prayer at mid-afternoon

	Standing	Bowing	Return to Standing	Prostration	Sitting	Return to Prostration	Return to Sitting
Rak'ah (1)							
Rak'ah (2)							
Rak'ah (3)							
Rak'ah (4)							

At the end of the prayer, turn your face to the right then left and say the Salaam

4. MAGHRIB

3 Rak'aat | Prayer at sunset

	Standing	Bowing	Return to Standing	Prostration	Sitting	Return to Prostration	Return to Sitting
Rak'ah (1)							
Rak'ah (2)							
Rak'ah (3)							

At the end of the prayer, turn your face to the right then left and say the Salaam

5. ISHA

4 Rak'aat | Prayer in the evening

	Standing	Bowing	Return to Standing	Prostration	Sitting	Return to Prostration	Return to Sitting
Rak'ah (1)							
Rak'ah (2)							
Rak'ah (3)							
Rak'ah (4)							

The 5 Daily Prayers Summarised

At the end of the prayer, turn your face to the right then left and say the Salaam

Pre-Prayer Checklist

○ **Wudu (Ablution)**

○ **Dress Code**

○ **Clean Area to Pray**

○ **Facing Qiblah**

○ **Niyyah (Intention)**

Dress Code

Boys should cover from the navel to the

knees and cover their shoulders.

Girls should cover all of their bodies

with loose clothing (hijab and jilbaab)

except for the face and hands.

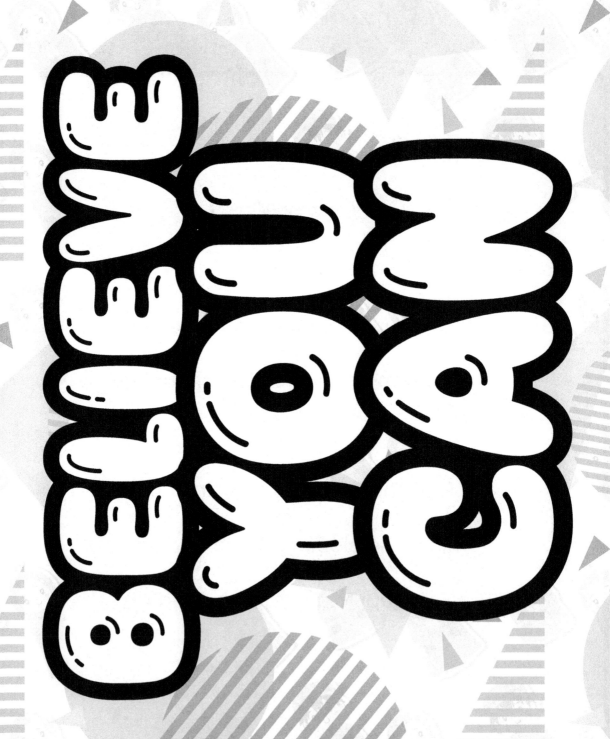

YOU AND ME LIVING

HOW TO PRAY STEP-BY-STEP

Before starting the prayer we begin by facing
the qiblah and making an intention from the
heart to pray to Allah.

Then we start the prayer with Takbir by raising
your hands towards your ears and saying:

اللهُ أَكْبَرُ

Allahu Akbar

(Allah is the Greatest)

Step ①

Takbir

Starting the Prayer

After saying takbir, move your hands and place them over your chest. Your right hand should be placed over the left, as shown. When we start our prayer, we start by saying the isti'adha:

أَعُوذُ بِاللَّهِ مِنَ الشَّيْطَانِ الرَّجِيمِ

Authubillahi minashaytaan-nirajeem

(I seek refuge in Allah from the cursed Satan)

Then we recite the Basmalah: (which is recited before every Surah)

بِسْمِ ٱللَّهِ ٱلرَّحْمَـٰنِ ٱلرَّحِيمِ

Bismillaahir Rahmaanir Raheem

(In the Name of Allah—the Most Compassionate, Most Merciful)

Then start reciting Surah Al-Fatihah and another Surah from the Qur'an. These Surahs can be found on the next few pages.

Step ②

Recite Surah Al-Fatihah along with another Surah

SURAH AL-FATIHAH

Chapter 1 in the Qur'an

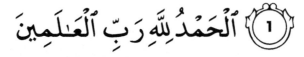

Alhamdu lillaahi Rabbil 'aalameen

(All praise is for Allah—Lord of all worlds,)

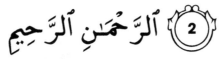

Ar-Rahmaanir-Raheem

(the Most Compassionate, Most Merciful,)

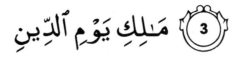

Maaliki Yawmid-Deen

(Master of the Day of Judgment)

SURAH AL-FATIHAH

Chapter 1 in the Qur'an

4 إِيَّاكَ نَعْبُدُ وَإِيَّاكَ نَسْتَعِينُ

Iyaa kana' budu wa iyaa kanasta-'een

(You (alone) we worship and You (alone) we ask for help.)

5 اهْدِنَا الصِّرَٰطَ الْمُسْتَقِيمَ

Ihdinas-Siraatal-Mustaqeem

(All praise is for Allah—Lord of all worlds,)

6 صِرَٰطَ الَّذِينَ أَنْعَمْتَ عَلَيْهِمْ غَيْرِ الْمَغْضُوبِ عَلَيْهِمْ وَلَا الضَّآلِّينَ

Siraatal-latheena an'amta 'alayhim ghayril-maghdoobi 'alayhim wa lad-daaalleen

(the Path of those You have blessed—not those You are displeased with, or those who are astray)

42

SURAH AL-KAWTHAR

Chapter 108 in the Qur'an

Innaaa a'taynaa kal kawtharr

(Indeed, We have granted you (O Prophet) abundant goodness)

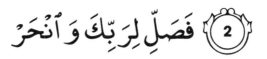

Fasalli li-rabbika wan harr

(So pray and sacrifice to your Lord (alone))

Inna shaani-aka huwal ab-tarr

(Only the one who hates you is truly cut off (from any goodness))

SURAH IKHLAAS

Chapter 112 in the Qur'an

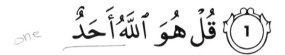

one

Qul huwallahu ahad

(Say, (O Prophet,) "He is Allah—One (and Indivisible);)

Allahussamad

(Allah—the Sustainer (needed by all))

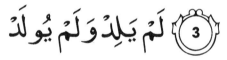

Lam yalid walam yoolad

(He has never had offspring, nor was He born)

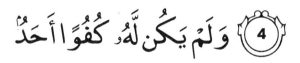

Walam yakullahu kufuwan ahad

(And there is none comparable to Him)

SURAH AL-FALAQ

Chapter 113 in the Qur'an

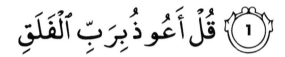

① قُلْ أَعُوذُ بِرَبِّ ٱلْفَلَقِ

Qul a'oothu bi rabbil-falaq

(Say, (O Prophet,) "I seek refuge in the Lord of humankind)

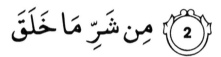

② مِن شَرِّ مَا خَلَقَ

Min sharri maa khalaq

(From the evil of whatever He has created,)

③ وَمِن شَرِّ غَاسِقٍ إِذَا وَقَبَ

Wa min sharri ghaasiqin ithaa waqab

(And from the evil of the night when it grows dark,)

④ وَمِن شَرِّ ٱلنَّفَّـٰثَـٰتِ فِى ٱلْعُقَدِ

Wa min sharrin-naffaa-thaati fil 'uqad

(And from the evil of those (witches casting spells by) blowing onto knots,)

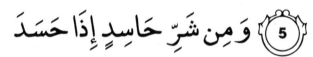

⑤ وَمِن شَرِّ حَاسِدٍ إِذَا حَسَدَ

Wa min sharri haasidin ithaa hasad

(And from the evil of an envier when they envy.")

45

SURAH AN-NAS

Chapter 114 in the Qur'an

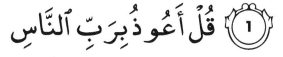

Qul a'oothu bi rabbin-naas

(Say, (O Prophet,) "I seek refuge in the Lord of humankind)

Ilaahin-naas

(The God of humankind)

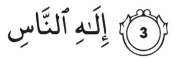

Malikin-naas

(The Master of humankind)

Min sharril waswaasil khannaas

(From the evil of the lurking whisperer)

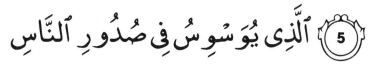

Allathee yu was wisu fee sudoorin-naas

(Who whispers into the hearts of humankind)

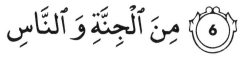

Minal jinnati wannaas

(From among jinn and humankind.")

46

As you are bending down say:

الله أُكْبَرُ

Allahu Akbar

(Allah is the Greateast)

Then keep your back straight and place your hands on your knees.

When you are in this position say quietly (x3):

سبُحانَ ربِّي العظيم

Subhaana rabbiyal adheem

(How perfect is my Lord, the Magnificent)

Step ③

Bow Down

Known as Ruku

As you are returning back to the standing position say:

سَمِعَ اللَّهُ لِمَنْ حَمِدَهُ

Sami Allahuliman hamida

(Allah hears those who praise Him)

Then say:

رَبَّنَا ولك الحمدُ

Rabbana walakal hamd

(Our Lord, to You is all praise)

Step ④

Return to Standing Position

As you are going down to the sujood position say:

اللهُ أَكْبَرُ

Allahu Akbar

(Allah is the Greateast)

And ensure that your forehead, nose, both palms, knees and toes are touching the ground (whilst keeping your elbows away from the floor).

When you are in this position say quietly (x3):

سُبْحَانَ رَبِّيَ الْأَعْلَى

Subhaana rabbiyal a'laa

(How perfect is my Lord, the Most High)

Step ⑤

Sujood

Also known as prostration

As you are rising up from sujood say:

اللهُ أَكْبَرُ

Allahu Akbar

(Allah is the Greateast)

When you are in the sitting position say:

رَّبِّ اغفِرلِي

Rabbigh-fir lee

(O my Lord, forgive me)

Step ⑥

Sitting

Sitting between 2 sujoods

Go down to the second sujood position say:

اللّٰهُ أَكْبَرُ

Allahu Akbar

(Allah is the Greateast)

When you are in this position you say quietly (x3):

سُبْحَانَ رَبِّيَ الْأَعْلَى

Subhaana rabbiyal a'laa

(How perfect is my Lord, the Most High)

Then rise from sujood to return to the standing position and say:

اللّٰهُ أَكْبَرُ

Allahu Akbar

(Allah is the Greateast)

Step ⑦

Second Sujood

Also known as second prostration

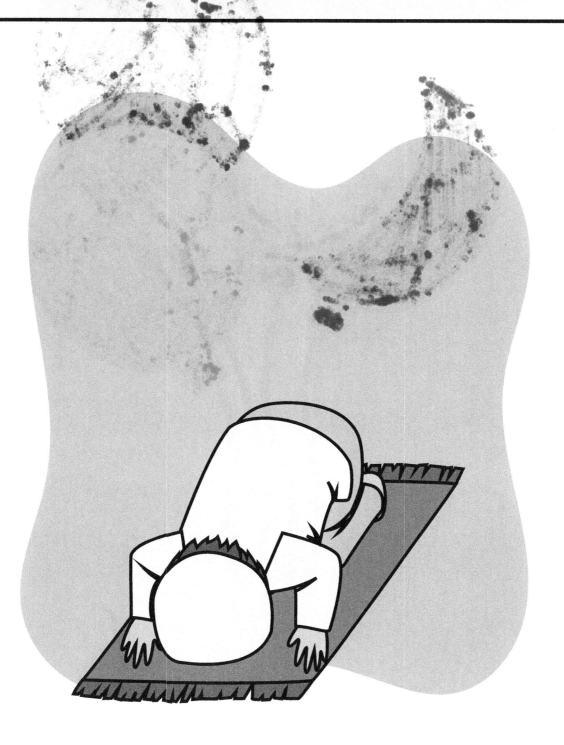

CONGRATS YOU JUST FINISHED ONE FULL RAKAAH!

EVERYTHING YOUR WAY

In the "second" rakaah of (Dhuhr, Asr, Maghrib

and Isha) we perform the same actions of the first

rakaah till we reach the second sujood position,

We rise from sujood and return back to our sitting

position and raise only your right index finger as

it's shown and then perform the "First" half of the

tashahhud which will learn together

Step ⑧

First Tashahhud

Performed in the second rakaah of Dhuhr, Asr, Maghrib and Isha

FIRST TASHAHHUD

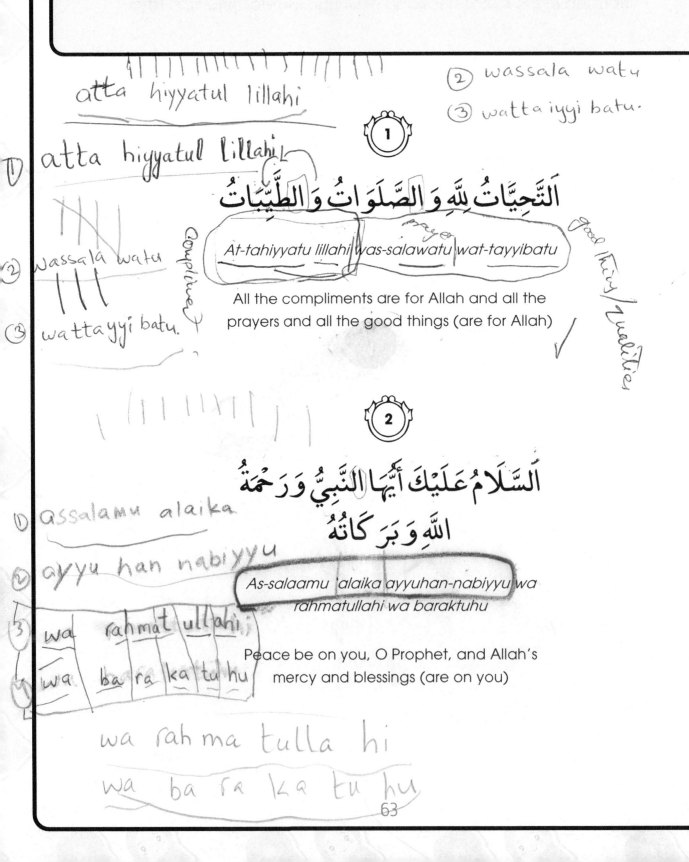

atta hiyyatul lillahi

② wassala watu

③ watta iyyi batu.

① atta hiyyatul lillahi

①

② Wassala watu

Compliment

③ wattayyi batu.

اَلتَّحِيَّاتُ لِلَّهِ وَ الصَّلَوَاتُ وَالطَّيِّبَاتُ

At-tahiyyatu lillahi was-salawatu wat-tayyibatu

All the compliments are for Allah and all the
prayers and all the good things (are for Allah)

good thing/qualities

②

اَلسَّلَامُ عَلَيْكَ أَيُّهَا النَّبِيُّ وَرَحْمَةُ
اللَّهِ وَبَرَكَاتُهُ

① assalamu alaika

② ayyu han nabiyyu

③ wa rahmat ullahi

④ wa ba ra ka tu hu

*As-salaamu 'alaika ayyuhan-nabiyyu wa
rahmatullahi wa baraktuhu*

Peace be on you, O Prophet, and Allah's
mercy and blessings (are on you)

wa rahma tulla hi

wa ba ra ka tu hu

63

FIRST TASHAHHUD

① Assalam o Alaina
② wa ala
③ Iba dillahi
④ Saliheen

③ ⓐ ② ①

السَّلَامُ عَلَيْنَا وَعَلَى عِبَادِ اللَّهِ الصَّالِحِينَ

As-salaamu 'alaina wa 'ala 'ibaadillahis-saaliheen

And peace be on us and on the good worshipers of Allah

wah da hu
la sha rik lahu

middle

④

Part 1 ✗

أَشْهَدُ أَنْ لَا إِلَهَ إِلَّا اللَّهُ وَحْدَهُ لَا شَرِيكَ لَهُ
وَأَشْهَدُ أَنَّ مُحَمَّدًا عَبْدُهُ وَرَسُولُهُ

Part 2

Ash-hadu an laa illaha illallahu wa ash-hadu anna muhammadan 'abduhu wa rasuluhu

I testify that none has the right to be worshipped but Allah and that Muhammad is His slave and Messenger

① Ash hadu Anlaa ilaha illatah

② Wahdahu la sharika lahu

③ wa ish hadu anna Muhammadan Abduhu
wa rasuluhu

64

In the "second" and "final" rakaah of (Fajr), in the "third" and "final" rakaah of (Maghrib) and in the "Fourth" and "final" rakaah of (Dhuhr, Asr and Isha), we perform the same actions of the first rakaah till we reach the second sujood position,

Then You will repeat step 7 ( ) again adding to the first tashahhud the rest of the tashahhud (full tashahhud)

Step ⑨

Final Tashahhud

Performed in the second rakaah of Fajr, the third rakaah of Maghrib and the fourth rakaah of Dhuhr Asr and Isha

FINAL TASHAHHUD

1

اللَّهُمَّ صَلِّ عَلَى مُحَمَّدٍ وَعَلَى آلِ مُحَمَّدٍ

Allahumma salli 'ala Muhammad wa 'ala aali Muhammad

O Allah! Praise Muhammad, and on the followers of Muhammad

2

كَمَا صَلَّيْتَ عَلَى إِبْرَاهِيمَ وَعَلَى آلِ إِبْرَاهِيمَ
إِنَّكَ حَمِيدٌ مَجِيدٌ

*Kamaa sallayta 'ala Ibraaheem wa 'ala aali Ibraaheem
innaka hameedun majeed*

As You Praised Ibraaheem, and the followers of Ibraaheem;
You are indeed Worthy of Praise, Full of Glory

FINAL TASHAHHUD

3

اللّٰهُمَّ بَارِكْ عَلَى مُحَمَّدٍ وَعَلَى آلِ مُحَمَّدٍ

Allahumma baarik ʿala Muhammad wa ʿala aali Muhammad

And send blessings on Muhammad, and on the followers of Muhammad

4

كَمَا بَارَكْتَ عَلَى إِبْرَاهِيمَ وَعَلَى آلِ إِبْرَاهِيمَ
إِنَّكَ حَمِيدٌ مَجِيدٌ

*Kamaa baarakta ʿala Ibraaheem wa ʿala aali Ibraaheem
innaka hameedun majeed*

As you sent blessings on Ibraaheem, and the followers of
Ibraaheem; You are indeed Worthy of Praise, Full of Glory

Do the first Tasleem by looking to the right and saying:

السَّلَامُ عَلَيْكُمْ وَرَحْمَةُ اللهِ وَبَرَكَاتُهُ

Assalaamu alaykum wa rahmatullah

(May peace and the mercy of God be upon you)

Step 10

The First Tasleem

Turning your head to the right side

Do the second Tasleem by looking to the left and saying:

السَّلاَمُ عَلَيْكُمْ وَرَحْمَةُ اللهِ وَبَرَكَاتُهُ

Assalaamu alaykum wa rahmatullah

(May peace and the mercy of God be upon you)

THE PRAYER IS COMPLETE! WELL DONE!

ARRANGE WUDU STEPS IN ORDER

◯ **Bismillah**

◯ **Clean nose**

◯ **Wipe head**

◯ **Wash hands**

- ⭘ **Clean ears**

- ⭘ **Wash face**

- ⭘ **Wash feet**

- ⭘ **Rinse mouth**

- ⭘ **Wash arms**

NAME THE PRAYER POSITION

_ _ _ _ _ _ _ _ _ _ _ _ _ _ _ _ _ _

_ _ _ _ _ _ _ _ _ _ _ _ _ _ _ _ _ _

_ _ _ _ _ _ _ _ _ _ _ _ _ _ _ _ _ _

_ _ _ _ _ _ _ _ _ _ _ _ _ _ _ _ _ _

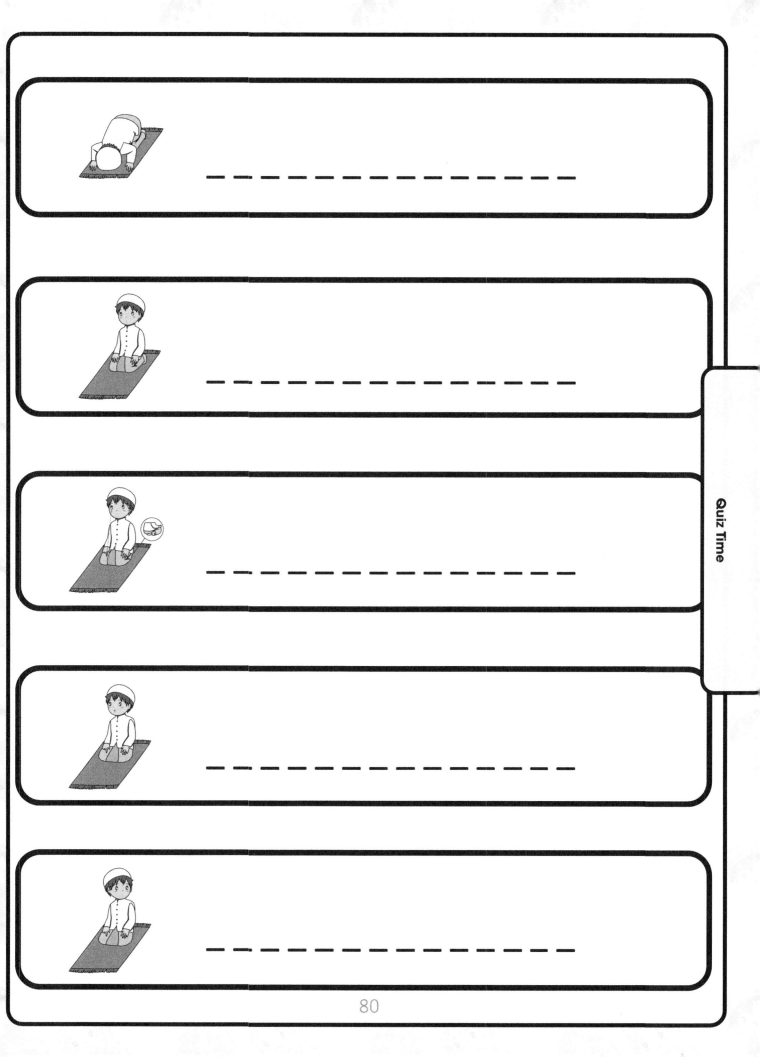

WRITE THE TIME OF EACH PRAYER

Fajr: _ _ _ _ _ _ _ _ _ _ _ _ _ _ _ _ _ _

Dhuhr: _ _ _ _ _ _ _ _ _ _ _ _ _ _ _ _ _ _

Asr: _ _ _ _ _ _ _ _ _ _ _ _ _ _ _ _ _ _

Maghrib: _ _ _ _ _ _ _ _ _ _ _ _ _ _ _ _ _ _

Isha: _ _ _ _ _ _ _ _ _ _ _ _ _ _ _ _ _ _

WRITE THE RAKAAT NUMBERS

○ **Fajr**

○ **Dhuhr**

○ **Asr**

○ **Maghrib**

○ **Isha**

30 DAY PRAYER LOG

30 DAY PRAYER LOG

Days	Fajr	Dhuhr	Asr	Maghrib	Isha
Day 1					
Day 2					
Day 3					
Day 4					
Day 5					

30 DAY PRAYER LOG

Days	Fajr	Dhuhr	Asr	Maghrib	Isha
Day 6					
Day 7					
Day 8					
Day 9					
Day 10					

30 DAY PRAYER LOG

Days	Fajr	Dhuhr	Asr	Maghrib	Isha
Day 11					
Day 12					
Day 13					
Day 14					
Day 15					

30 DAY PRAYER LOG

Days	Fajr	Dhuhr	Asr	Maghrib	Isha
Day 16					
Day 17					
Day 18					
Day 19					
Day 20					

30 Day Prayer Log

30 DAY PRAYER LOG

Days	Fajr	Dhuhr	Asr	Maghrib	Isha
Day 21					
Day 22					
Day 23					
Day 24					
Day 25					

30 DAY PRAYER LOG

Days	Fajr	Dhuhr	Asr	Maghrib	Isha
Day 26					
Day 27					
Day 28					
Day 29					
Day 30					

NEVER FORGET HOW MUCH

If you liked this book, you will love our other books!

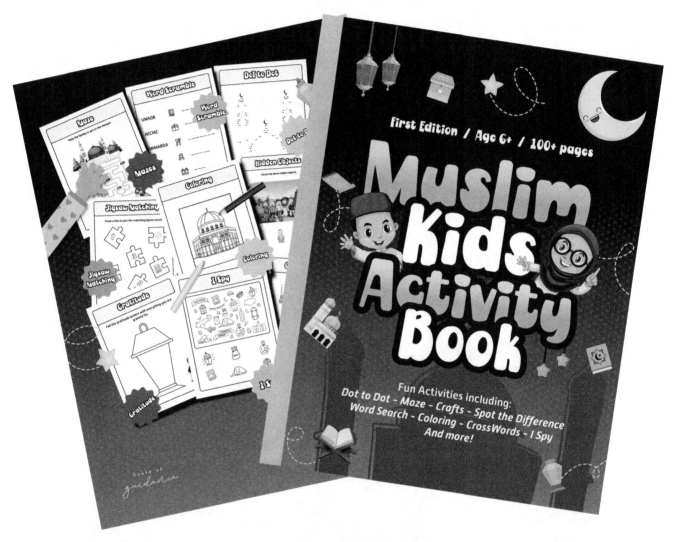

Muslim Kids Activity Book

If you're looking for an entertaining activity book for your child to enjoy as a productive yet fun pass time!

This book is perfect for Ramadan, Eid, Special Occasions, and even any time throughout the year!

PERFECT FOR ALL KIDS AGES 6+ WITH ACTIVITIES SUCH AS:

Word Search, Crosswords, Coloring, Dot to Dot, Object Matching, Jigsaw Matching, Mazes, Word Scramble, I Spy, Hidden Objects, Spot the Difference, Drawing Prompts, Create Your Own Story, Alphabetical Order, Find the Hadith, 30 Day Salah Log, 30 Day Quran Log & Gratitude Journal!

You can find all of our books on Amazon!

If you liked this book, you will love our other books!

Quran Verse Colouring Book

If you're looking for an **STRESS-RELIEVING COLORING BOOK** for yourself to enjoy as a productive, fun and educational pass time then look no further than this **QURAN VERSE COLORING BOOK** filled with mandala patterns and mindful designs on every page!

There are a total of **30 famous and well-known verses** contained in this book for you to enjoy!

PERFECT GIFT FOR ADULTS AND TEENS TOO!

This book is **A PERFECT GIFT** for Ramadan, Eid, Special Occasions, and even **ANY TIME THROUGHOUT THE YEAR!**

You can find all of our books on Amazon!

If you liked this book, you will love our other books!

Muslim Gratitude Journal
A Complete 52 Week Guide To Building A Grateful Mindset And Positive Relationship With Allah

This Muslim Gratitude Journal has been designed with the modern-day Muslim in mind. Our busy lives can sometimes prevent us from nurturing our connection with Allah.

For this reason, we devised this journal to help you to begin cultivating an attitude of gratitude with your Creator in mind.

We've designed 160+ beautiful pages for you to help build mindfulness and thankfulness. Every page has plenty of space to write in with stylish Islamic floral patterns!

The 30 Day Muslim Gratitude Journal
A Fully Immersive Journaling Experience with Thought-Provoking, Unique Prompts Every Single Day!

This journal is designed to help the Muslim reader construct and fortify an attitude of gratitude within one month (or just 30 days!)

Showing gratitude to Allah is one of the core, if not the ultimate, reason why we have been created.

It is for this reason we believe it to be even more important in modern society to build a grateful mindset so we can ultimately be more thankful towards our Creator for all the blessings he has given us, and constantly gives us on a daily basis.

You can find all of our books on Amazon!

If you liked this book, you will love our other books!

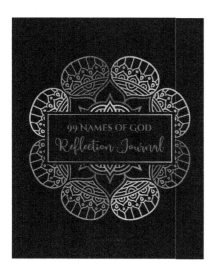

99 Names of God Reflection Journal
Learn, Reflect and Contemplate The 99 Names of Your Creator Daily - Suitable for Muslims & Non-Muslims

This book shares the commonly known Names that our Creator revealed to us 1400 years ago. It was designed for Muslims and Non-Muslims to help the reader build a stronger bond with their Creator.

Included on every page spread is the Name (in English and Arabic), the meaning, and 3 boxes to write inside titled; 'This Name makes me feel...', 'My notes...' and 'How I will use this Name to call upon my Creator...'.

**Islamic Phrases
Lined Notebooks**

You can find all of our books on Amazon!

Printed in Great Britain
by Amazon

26506873R00057